LIVING MY BEST LIFE

CUTE & GIRLY COLOURING BOOK

Amelia Green

AF746582

A LITTLE NOTE FROM AMELIA GREEN

Thank you so much for choosing this colouring book!
I hope it brings you a moment of calm, creativity, and joy.

If you'd like to show us your coloured pages,
post a pic or video and tag us.

Curious how we colour the pages or looking for fresh ideas?
Come hang out on TikTok and Instagram.

tiktok.com/@AmeliaGreenColoring

instagram.com/AmeliaGreenColoring

Now grab your favourite pens, get comfy, and let's make the
world a little more colourful, one page at a time!

COLOUR TEST PAGE

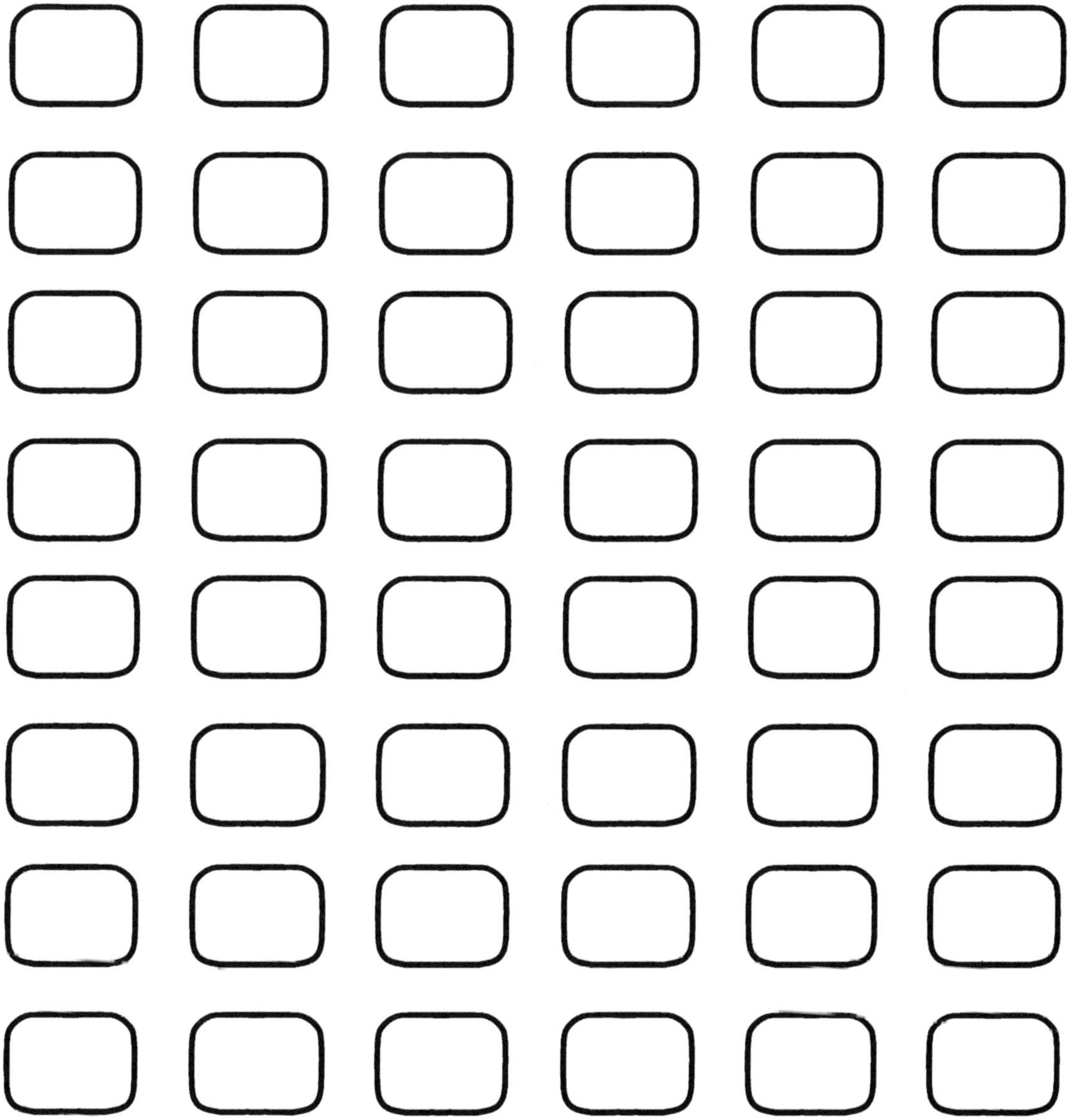

This book is printed on quality paper, but if you use alcohol-based markers, we recommend that you insert a sheet behind the page to protect subsequent pages.

FLOWERS

GOALS
DREAMS

CAFE

LIFE IS
BETTER
WITH
BOOKS
BEST
PRICE

PENGUIN BOOKS

UK | USA | Canada | Ireland | Australia
India | New Zealand | South Africa | China

Penguin Random House Australia

Penguin Random House Australia is part of the Penguin Random House group of companies whose addresses can be found at global.penguinrandomhouse.com.

First published by Penguin, an imprint of Penguin Random House Australia Pty Ltd, in 2026

Printed in China

NATIONAL LIBRARY OF AUSTRALIA

A catalogue record for this book is available from the National Library of Australia

ISBN 978 1 76162 073 7 (Paperback)

penguin.com.au

We at Penguin Random House Australia acknowledge that Aboriginal and Torres Strait Islander
peoples are the Traditional Custodians and the first storytellers of the lands on which we live and work. We honour Aboriginal and Torres Strait Islander peoples' continuous connection to Country, waters, skies and communities. We celebrate Aboriginal and Torres Strait Islander stories, traditions and living cultures; and we pay our respects to Elders past and present.